THE BOOK OF LOVE

VOL.1

BY LISA LAYNE & PAUL SINN

A Fireside Book
Published by Simon & Schuster, Inc., New York

FIRESIDE and colophon are registered trademarks
of Simon & Schuster, Inc.

Designed by Galarneau & Sinn, Ltd.

Manufactured in the United States of America

1   2   3   4   5   6   7   8   9   10

ISBN: 0-671-50056-2

XXXOOO to the following, who
graciously granted us permission
to reprint copyrighted material for
the 366 Days of Love calendar, and
again for this book:

Harry N. Abrams, Inc., for excerpt
from The Art of Advertising: George
Lois on Mass Communication,
© 1977 by Harry N. Abrams, B. V.,
The Netherlands, published by
Harry N. Abrams, Inc., in New York,
all rights reserved; The New York
Times for excerpts from selected
issues © 1956, 1971, 1980 by The
New York Times Company, reprinted
by permission; Random House for
excerpt from Ulysses by James
Joyce, © 1914 by Margaret Caroline
Anderson and renewed 1942, 1946
by Nora Joseph Joyce, reprinted by
permission of Random House, Inc.;
The Bodley Head for Ulysses permis-
sion for Canada; The Editors of Roll-
ing Stone for excerpt from The Ballad
of John and Yoko by Rolling Stone
Press © 1982, all rights reserved,
reprinted by permission; David
Thomson for quote which appeared
in Film Comment; Viking Penguin,
Inc., for excerpt from Finnegan s
Wake by James Joyce, © 1939 by
James Joyce, copyright renewed
1967 by George Joyce and Lucia
Joyce, reprinted by permission of
Viking Penguin, Inc.

To: **LADSON**

- ☑ With love.
- ☑ XXXOOO
- ☐ You're wonderful.
- ☐ I want you.
- ☐ Thanks for a wonderful evening.
- ☐ Thanks for the memories.
- ☑ You're so bad.
- ☐ You're so good.
- ☐ (Sigh...)
- ☐ Fondly.
- ☑ Passionately.
- ☑ Forever.
- ☑ And ever.
- ☐ I think I'm in love. Again.

From: **MARY. (&PAUL SINN)**

> **Not to worry. The personals have quietly but steadily become the province of people who are probably pretty much like you.**

Lindsy Van Gelder in the August 1983 *Ms.* magazine article entitled "Love Among the Classifieds: A Take-Charge Way to Meet New People." Van Gelder sets down many helpful hints to keep in mind while composing an ad. "The idea isn't to garner a zillion responses," she says. "If you're looking to cut a wide swath, buy yourself something red and low-cut and go back to the bars."

DWJMCFGbiB SEEKS ABC

How to decipher a personal classfied ad

These letters have evolved over a twenty-year period as the shorthand in *Village Voice* personal ads and have become the standard for writing and deciphering personals everywhere.

S—single (Can also mean *straight*. Read ad for context.). **M**—male (Can also mean *married*. Read ad for context.). **B**—black. **W**—white. **F**—female. **J**—Jewish. **C**—Christian. **bi**—bisexual. **G**—gay. **D**—divorced.

People who answer personals say that advertisers have a tendency to exaggerate. Here, based on their observations, is an informal glossary of what the words really mean:

"Early 30's": at least 50; *"mature"*: early 70's; *"tall"*: 5'1"; *"articulate"*: very nervous; *"physically active"*: doesn't mean sports; *"loves racquetball, tennis, skiing, backpacking"*: watches a lot of TV; *"seeks commitment"*: usually with multiple partners simultaneously.

The first known marriage ad appeared on July 19, 1695, in an English journal and read, in part:

OPPORTUNITIES

A GENTLEMAN about 30 Years of Age, that says he has a Very Good Estate, would willingly Match Himself to some young Gentlewoman that has a fortune of £3000 or thereabouts…

Ad from an eighteenth-century English magazine:

LOST & FOUND

WHEREAS a tall young Gentleman above the common size, dress'd in yellow-grounded flowered velvet… was narrowly observed and much approved of by a certain young lady at the last Ridotto. This is to acquaint the said young Gentleman, if his heart is entirely disengaged, that if he will apply to A.B. at Garaway Coffee House, he may be directed to have an interview with the said young lady, which may prove greatly to his advantage.

ANNOUNCEMENT

WHEN A WOMAN NAMED Helen Morison advertised for a husband in the *Manchester Weekly Journal* in 1727, townspeople were so outraged that the lord mayor had the woman committed to an insane asylum for a month.

Personal Ad Portraits

biWJM SEEKS BGDCF

Lonny Shavelson has written and taken the photographs for a book about people who look for relationships through personal classified ads. He found the subjects for his book, *Personal Ad Portraits*, by answering a cross-section of personal classifieds and asking permission to include the ad writers in his book. Shavelson published the book himself because he was afraid a large publisher might market it as an exposé. *Personal Ad Portraits* is scheduled for national distribution and is available from DeNovo Press, P.O. Box 5106, Berkeley, CA 94705.

I have not had a facelift. The only reason I look younger today than I did ten years ago is because of what my wife has discovered.

—Caption under photo of a cuddling Ernest and Tova Borgnine in an ad for Tova's "Amazing New Formula From Beverly Hills [that] Lets You Take Up To 10 Years Off Your Looks Without The Scars And Expense Of Plastic Surgery."

PUT YOUR HEAD ON MY SHOULDER.

—Early 1960's love song by Paul Anka, transformed into theme of 1983 dandruff shampoo commercial.

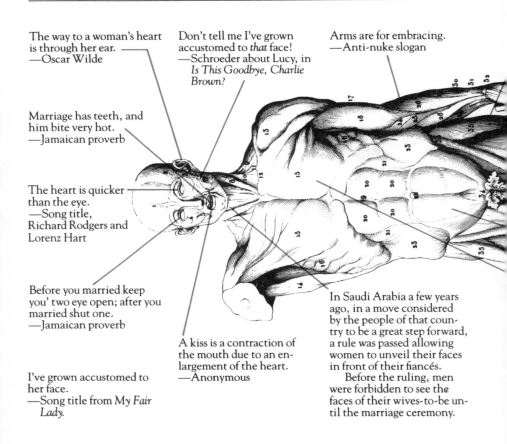

The way to a woman's heart is through her ear.
—Oscar Wilde

Don't tell me I've grown accustomed to *that* face!
—Schroeder about Lucy, in *Is This Goodbye, Charlie Brown?*

Arms are for embracing.
—Anti-nuke slogan

Marriage has teeth, and him bite very hot.
—Jamaican proverb

The heart is quicker than the eye.
—Song title, Richard Rodgers and Lorenz Hart

Before you married keep you' two eye open; after you married shut one.
—Jamaican proverb

A kiss is a contraction of the mouth due to an enlargement of the heart.
—Anonymous

I've grown accustomed to her face.
—Song title from *My Fair Lady.*

In Saudi Arabia a few years ago, in a move considered by the people of that country to be a great step forward, a rule was passed allowing women to unveil their faces in front of their fiancés.

Before the ruling, men were forbidden to see the faces of their wives-to-be until the marriage ceremony.

According to a London *Sunday Times* poll, men think women admire a muscular chest and shoulders above all other male attributes. But the poll of women revealed they like "small and sexy buttocks" most of all. Muscular chest and shoulders ranked tenth out of a list of eleven.

In a *Glamour* magazine poll, on the other hand, women said they looked for a nice face first of all. Other physical findings from *Glamour*: Women like brown, curly hair, blue eyes, mustaches, nice smiles, and hairy chests.

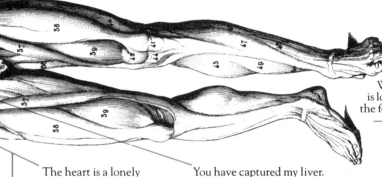

What they call "heart" is located far lower than the fourth waistcoat button.
—Georg Lichtenberg

The heart is a lonely hunter.
—Title of a novel by Carson McCullers

When there is room in the heart there is room in the house.
—Danish proverb

You have captured my liver.
—In the Berber tribe of Morocco, women say this to men as a signal they want to marry them. A healthy liver promotes good digestion and happiness and is therefore considered the center of love, instead of the heart.

What you see is what you get.
—Flip Wilson
(as Geraldine)

French emperor Napoleon married his love, Josephine, on March 9, 1796. On their wedding night, Josephine's dog, thinking Napoleon was attacking her, jumped on the bed and bit him.

Lovebirds are:
a) Parrots
b) Parakeets
c) Doves
d) Swallows

If you value fidelity in a love partner, you can't do better than to marry a Buffalo.
—An Nguyen,
Chinese Astrology

Love is that delightful interval between meeting a beautiful girl and discovering that she looks like a haddock.
—John Barrymore

Love me, love my dog.
—John Heywood.

I DO. ARF!

At a wedding several years ago in Indiana, the guests were seated, the bride walked down the aisle, and the theme from *Benji* was played. After that, three impeccably groomed dogs walked in and took their seats in the front row.

This did not surprise any of the other guests, who knew the groom was a dog obedience trainer.

Male turkeys gobble and strut during mating season to attract hens. They are polygamous creatures, but harems of more than six hens are rare.

Marjorie Workhoven, manager of the Circus Circus Chapel of the Fountain in Las Vegas (see *Love & Marriage & Divorce*), once owned the Chateaux Chapel in Los Angeles. In 1978 the Chateaux made arrangements for the marriage of two dachshunds. The $1,000 tab included chapel, vocalist, champagne, a cake baked in the shape of a dog bone, and, at the end of each pew, a plastic fire hydrant decorated with ribbons.

That's a Moray.

Martha Giles of Newark, New Jersey, filed suit for divorce in April 1949 on the grounds that her husband had attacked her with a live eel.

Dr. Theresa Crenshaw, a sex therapist and clinical professor at the University of California, San Diego School of Medicine, believes that commercial aphrodisiacs will be on the market within ten years.

"We will have pills you can take to treat premature ejaculation and psychological impotence," she told *San Diego* magazine. Dr. Crenshaw has received a grant from a drug company to research a drug they suspect has aphrodisiac properties.

She thinks one of the reasons we haven't had hard facts about aphrodisiacs before is because "serious scientific researchers have not looked for them."

Canadian researchers recently tested yohimbine, a chemical derived from the African yohimbe tree, on twenty-three men suffering from impotence related to physical problems. According to *Time* magazine, ten of the men showed a noticeable improvement, and six were able to reach orgasm. ♥

Several perfume manufacturers are incorporating pheromones into their scents. Pheromones are a type of chemical long used in scientific applications—as a sex attractant in insect traps, for example. They may evoke lusty behavior in humans, too.

Jovan makes one such perfume, Andron, with a different scent each for men and women. Dollar sales for 1983 were expected to be in the millions. ♥

While sales of aphrodisiac-like perfumes soar into the millions, "Boar Mate" is raking in only $150,000 a year.

No wonder; Boar Mate simulates the odor of a sexually aroused male pig and smells like "musty, dirty, sweaty socks," according to its U.S. distributor.

A British invention, Boar Mate was designed to help hog farmers increase pig production. A two-second spritz of the stuff under a sow's nose during the peak of heat is all it takes to bring on arousal and, subsequently, plenty of little pigs.

Boar Mate apparently affects people, too. British researchers sprayed it on selected chairs in a London hospital waiting room and found that arriving women picked those chairs over all others. ♥

Moneysworth magazine reported in 1979 that Indian doctors studying ancient Hindu medicine had discovered the formula for effective aphrodisiacs. The article said plans were in the offing to make the aphrodisiacs available in do-it-yourself kits to India's 650 million people, who constitute a population second in size only to China. ♥

What is a "love apple"?
a) Potato
b) Avocado
c) Tomato
d) Gravenstein apple

Answer: c   The Spanish, who brought tomato seeds to us from South America, believed the vegetable to be an aphrodisiac.

To make sex sexier, the ancient Greeks consumed hyena udder, eighteenth century Italian lover Giovanni Casanova (see *Love & Literature*) ate oysters, and the early Chinese were said to have eaten ginseng and rhinoceros horn. Present-day edibles believed to induce lust, if not love, include bananas, figs, clams, tomatoes, avocados, onions, asparagus, and the Japanese raw fish delicacy *sushi*. ♥

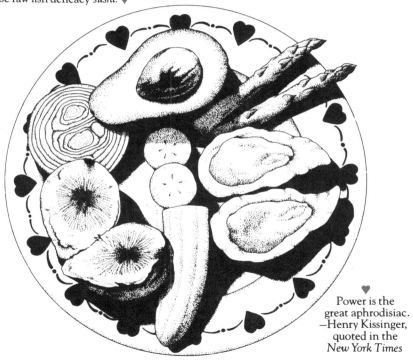

♥
Power is the great aphrodisiac.
—Henry Kissinger, quoted in the *New York Times*

Artist Wendy Clarke has made more than 1,000 video tapes of Americans saying whatever comes to mind—or heart—about love. Each person is given three minutes for an impromptu "speech." Samples: "I love my godchild and my friends, but there are other kinds of love." And, "There are lovers of all kinds but I am the biggest and best of all."

The Love Tapes have been shown at the Museum of Modern Art in New York. Clarke plans to take them around the world and make tapes of people in other countries, including the Soviet Union. Contributions to help finance the trip may be sent to the non-profit organization Peopletapes, 24 Horatio Street, New York, NY 10014.

THE GREATER THE MAN'S SOUL, THE DEEPER HE LOVES.
—Leonardo da Vinci

When Rodin's sculpture "The Kiss" came to Tokyo in the 1920's, it was considered so risque it was hidden behind a bamboo curtain.

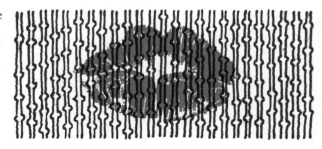

THE MERCEDES IN YOU BRINGS OUT THE JAG IN ME

A Silicon Valley computer chip salesman has come up with the idea to match people through license plate numbers on their cars.

Barry Lorenzo thought of it while stuck in commuter traffic and became convinced that there were others like him who see attractive people in cars "without a way in the world to make contact."

Lorenzo thinks the setup might be ideal for singles tired of making the rounds of bars. How it would work: You'd send Lorenzo's company (tentatively called Fantasy's) $5 and a car license plate number and, in return, you'd get the occupant's name and address.

A FUNNY THING HAPPENED ON THE WAY TO...

According to the London *Sunday Mirror*, a half-naked man was immobilized by a slipped disc while he and a woman were necking in a sports car in Regent's Park, London. The woman, trapped beneath him, managed to honk the horn with her foot to summon help. Firemen had to cut through the car frame to free the couple. The distraught woman's main concern was how to tell her husband what had happened to his car.

THROUGH THICK AND THIN.

CHAUCER
CERVANTES
SPENSER
DRYDEN
COWPER
BUTLER

For a love relationship to work, there has to be agreement between partners of what to expect from that relationship, say psychologists. The commitment may be different from relationship to relationship but it must be there. Anthropologists have noted that ritual is vital in maintaining good relationships as well. A ritual can be as formal as having weekly lunch with a friend, or as subtle as kissing a partner goodbye in the morning, joking, handshaking, or hugging.

If you love somebody you got nothing but trouble. So you either stop loving 'em, or love 'em a whole lot more.

—Colonel Potter to Max Klinger in the last episode of "M*A*S*H"

After his divorce, Walter Davis enlisted the aid of a London computerized marriage service to find him a new love. Out of thousands of possibilities, the computer came up with Ethel, his former wife. They were re-married in 1975.

I want a companion who is small and attractive, loves water sports, is fond of sea-food, and enjoys group activities. —Request to a computer dating service. The reply, according to *New Woman* magazine: "Marry a penguin."

The first marriage part-ners to be matched by computer were intro-duced on Art Linkletter's TV show *People Are Funny*, and married October 18, 1958, in Hollywood.

The first computer to perform marriages is an Apple in Sunnyvale, California. It interrupts the ceremony with the command, "Press space bar to continue." And instead of saying "I do," bride and groom must press "y" for yes. The Apple's human counterpart, Reverend Ron, conceived the idea for the deaf. Though there have been no bites from deaf people, digital weddings have caught on. The Rev and his Apple have graduated to full-blown church weddings complete with computer-controlled synthesized music.

LOVE & DEATH

LOVE & **DISAGREEMENTS**

LET'S HEAR IT FOR KRAMER VS. KRAMER

If parents hide disagreements, their children are likely to become adults who cannot deal with conflict.

So believes Selma Kramer, professor and head of child psychiatry at the Medical College of Pennsylvania.

In a Knight-Ridder news story, Kramer told how, many years ago, she and her husband presented a "united front" to their children, strongly agreeing not to disagree in their presence—a widely held belief in those days.

She notes that her daughter grew up thinking it abnormal to have arguments and found it hard to feel comfortable about arguing with her own husband.

Kramer Sr. is certain now that it's "healthy if kids know that parents can disagree and make up." She says they grow up accepting that people can love each other and still disagree. And they tend to be more autonomous in their own thinking.

What did Scarlett say that prompted Rhett to reply, "Frankly, my dear, I don't give a damn"?
a) The Yankees are at the front door.
b) The house is burning down.
c) If you go what shall I do?
d) If you go bankrupt what shall I do?

Answer: c   In the book, Rhett actually said, "My dear, I don't give a damn."

MISS PAGET: I WOULDN'T *DREAM* OF MARRYING YOU.
JOE: **THAT SUITS ME.**
            —*A Town Like Alice*

Tips on how to have an argument as reported in Ms. magazine by Susan Starr Richards:
**Don't try to sound reasonable.
Don't be afraid to do battle over nothing. Most big fights are about nothing.
Crying's okay as long as you're not crying because you can't say what you really mean.
No hitting.
Don't say irrevocable things. Most people can feel a physical twinge when they think of something that will *really* hurt the other person. Take this twinge as a danger signal.**
Says Richards on sulking: "The man who makes a habit of sulking for days after a fight, giving you the silent treatment or being curt or coolly polite or sorrowful, withholding the usual forms of affection, is interested in getting his way, not fighting; interested in power, not love; and is possibly too chicken to bother living with. Make your plans accordingly."

GEORGE: STOP IT, MARTHA.
MARTHA: LIKE HELL I WILL.
        —*Who's Afraid of Virginia Woolf?*

I'LL BE DAMNED IF I'LL LOVE JUST TO LOVE—THERE'S GOT TO BE MORE TO IT THAN THAT.

—Humphrey Bogart

Which song did Sam play in the movie *Casablanca*?
a) "Here's Looking at You"
b) "Round Up the Usual Suspects"
c) "A Kiss Is a Kiss"
d) "As Time Goes By"

Answer: d

Richard Gere? And all these years I've been trying to act like Alan Alda! What do women want?

—Letter from a *Newsweek* reader about the cover story on male idols, which featured actor Richard Gere.

When playwright Charles MacArthur met actress Helen Hayes at a party, he offered her a bowl of salted peanuts and said, "I wish they were emeralds."

"That was the end of my heart," Hayes said years later. "I never got it back."

Which movie had a scene with two lovers embracing on the beach while the waves washed over them?   a) *Airplane*
b) *From Here to Eternity*   c) *10*   d) All of the above

Answer: d

A miserable marriage can wobble along for years until something comes along and pushes one of the people over the brink…For me, it was a whole production staff and camera crew.

—Pat Loud, *A Woman's Story*, about the 1974 documentary "An American Family," which chronicled the breakup of her family.

5 MOVIES TO SEE (AND 5 T

—Roger Ebert, movie critic, *Chic*

To see:
1. Singin' in the Rain
2. Amarcord
3. Casablanca
4. Heartland
5. The Return of Martin Guerre

I believe to this day that the Louds self-destructed on camera because they felt it was what we wanted to see, what we required to grant them fame.

—Television critic Ron Miller

What the Louds are doing today:
Kevin Loud, 30, is a Houston oil company employee.
Lance Loud, 31, is a rock singer.
Grant Loud, 29, is a ballad singer.
Delilah Loud, 26, works in advertising in Los Angeles.
After Pat Loud divorced husband Bill, she moved to New York, where she works as a literary agent.
None of the Loud children have married.

A recent *Paris Match* survey revealed that French men would choose actress Catherine Deneuve over all others as the ideal partner in an affair. French women chose actor Alain Delon.

VOID) ON THE FIRST DATE

-Times and *At the Movies*, NBC.

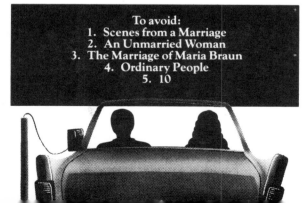

To avoid:
1. **Scenes from a Marriage**
2. **An Unmarried Woman**
3. **The Marriage of Maria Braun**
4. **Ordinary People**
5. **10**

I LOVE LUCY'S 10 BEST

1. Job switching in Kramer's Kandy Kitchen.
2. Lucy does a TV commercial called "Vitameatavegamin."
3. The Ricardos and Mertzes buy the restaurant, "A Little Bit of Cuba, a Big Hunk of America."
4. Lucy and Ethel do the women-from-Mars publicity stunt.
5. Lucy writes the novel, *Real Gone with the Wind.*
6. Lucy and Ethel wallpaper the bedroom.
7. Lucy does a fashion show in Los Angeles with Hollywood wives.
8. Lucy and Ethel go into the salad dressing business.
9. Harpo Marx pays Lucy a surprise visit.
10. Lucy and Ethel visit Grauman's Chinese Theatre and steal John Wayne's footprints.

—Susan Bailey, *I Love Lucy* fanatic

"The most wonderful feeling I suppose I've ever experienced in my life," was how James Hahn of Cape Girardeau, Missouri, described being reunited in 1983 with identical triplet brothers after fifty-seven years.

The trio were adopted in infancy by different families, and had chance encounters over the years but didn't know they were brothers. They now marvel over similarities: All experience ringing in their ears, fear heights, love singing, and were allergic to milk as youngsters.

IN THE ALL-IMPORTANT WORLD OF FAMILY RELATIONS, THERE ARE OTHER WORDS ALMOST AS POWERFUL AS THE FAMOUS "I LOVE YOU." THEY ARE "MAYBE YOU'RE RIGHT." **—OWEN ARNOLD**

Children begin by loving their parents; as they grow older they judge them; sometimes they forgive them.
—Oscar Wilde, *A Woman of No Importance*

When will the arms race cease? When we love our children more than we fear each other.
—Member of an American debating team speaking in Russia, "A Journey to Russia," *Front Line*, PBS.

WHEN A FATHER GIVES TO HIS SON, BOTH LAUGH; WHEN A SON GIVES TO HIS FATHER, BOTH CRY.

—Yiddish proverb

WE JUST HAPPEN TO LIKE CHILDREN.

—Woman quoted on the birth of her eighteenth child, 1959.

In honor of her own and other mothers, Anna Jarvis proposed the wearing of a white carnation and the holding of special church services every second Sunday in May.

Mother's Day was first observed on May 8, 1907, the anniversary of Anna's mother's death.

Congress gave official recognition in 1914.

The thing that impresses me most about America is the way parents obey their children.
—Duke of Windsor, quoted in *Look* magazine

The idea for Father's Day originated with a woman in Spokane, Washington, who was inspired by her father. He raised her and five brothers after the early death of his wife. Father's Day was first observed in 1910.

Thanks, Dad.

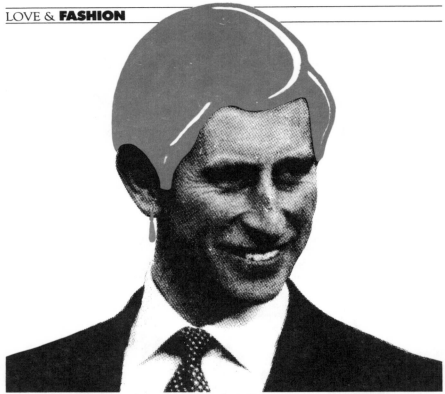

Men who wear earrings and toupees are least desirable to women, according to a survey conducted by the British magazine *Woman*. Ninety-two percent of the respondents said they would turn down a man who wore a pair of earrings, while seventy-three percent said no to even one earring. Only five percent said they would consider a man with a toupee.

HE GAVE HER A LOOK YOU COULD HAVE POURED ON A WAFFLE. —RING LARDNER

RESEARCHERS HAVE OBSERVED THAT PEOPLE WHO MAKE A HABIT OF FALLING IN AND OUT OF LOVE ALSO TEND TO HAVE CRAVINGS FOR CHOCOLATE.

THE FEELING OF FRIENDSHIP IS LIKE THAT OF BEING COMFORTABLY FILLED WITH A MEAL; LOVE, LIKE BEING ENLIVENED WITH CHAMPAGNE. —SAMUEL JOHNSON

AND WE MEET, WITH CHAMPAGNE AND A CHICKEN, AT LAST.—LADY MARY WORTLEY MONTAGU

AT EARLY ROMAN WEDDINGS, THE BRIDE AND GROOM SHARED A SLICE OF BARLEY CAKE. THE GROOM BROKE THE REMAINDER OVER THE BRIDE'S HEAD, SYMBOLIZING THE BREAKING OF THE HYMEN.

LOVE IS AS UNEXPECTED AS SQUIRT FROM AGGRESSIVE GRAPEFRUIT.—CHARLIE CHAN

WHERE CAN YOU FIND THE PHRASE, "WE HAVE A LOT IN COMMON"? A) GIRL SCOUT COOKIE BOX. B) OVER THE ENTRANCE OF THE FOUR SEASONS RESTAURANT IN NEW YORK. C) ON THE DEDICATION PAGE OF *THE JOY OF COOKING* COOKBOOK. D) TATTOOED ON THE UPPER PART OF CHEF PAUL PRUDHOMME'S RIGHT ARM. A :ЯƎWSИA

A LOVING CUP IS A LARGE TWO-HANDLED DRINKING VESSEL, USUALLY SILVER, PASSED AMONG FRIENDS AND GUESTS AT THE CLOSE OF A BANQUET. FIRST USAGE OF THE TERM, ACCORDING TO THE *OXFORD ENGLISH DICTIONARY*, WAS IN THE NOVEMBER 9, 1808, MINUTES OF THE COMMITTEE FOR THE LORD MAYOR'S BANQUET.

It all comes down to who does the dishes. —NORMAN MAILER

Friend…GOOD.
—Frankenstein monster, in
The Bride of Frankenstein

Let me live in my house by
the side of the road and be a
friend of man.
—Sam Foss, *The House by
the Side of the Road*

The only way to have a
friend is to be one.
—Ralph Waldo Emerson

Friendship is seldom lasting
but between equals.
—Samuel Johnson

In our limited conditions of
life nothing enhances our
security so much as
friendship.
—Epicurus

Whoever wants me as I am
is content.
—Ghana proverb

We forgive more faults in
love than in friendship.
—Jean de La Bruyère

The more we love our friends,
the less we flatter them; it is
by excusing nothing that
pure love shows itself.
—Moliere

We take care of our health,
we lay up our money, we
make our roof tight and our
clothing sufficient, but who
provides wisely that he shall
not be wanting in the best
property of all—friends?
—Ralph Waldo Emerson

Friends are people who
borrow my books and set
wet glasses on them.
—Edwin Arlington Robinson

Place names
containing love:

LOVELAND
OHIO

LOVE
SASKATCHEWAN

LOVELAND
COLORADO

LOVELOCK
NEVADA

LOVELAND
OKLAHOMA

LOVELADY
TEXAS

LOVE CANAL
NEW YORK

LOVE
MISSISSIPPI

LOVE COUNTY
OKLAHOMA

LOVELAND
IOWA

LOVE POINT
MARYLAND

NO MAN
IS AN ISLAND.
—JOHN DONNE

The original wedding anniversary gift list called for presents every five years or so. In 1937, the American National Retail Jewelers Association expanded the list to include the following:

1st	—Paper	11th	—Steel
2nd	—Cotton	12th	—Silk
3rd	—Leather	13th	—Lace
4th	—Linen	14th	—Ivory
5th	—Wood	15th	—Crystal
6th	—Iron	20th	—China
7th	—Wool	25th	—Silver
8th	—Bronze	30th	—Pearl
9th	—Pottery	35th	—Coral
10th	—Tin	40th	—Ruby
		45th	—Sapphire
		50th	—Gold
		55th	—Emerald
		60th	—Diamond

**FORTUNE DOTH
GIVE THESE PAIRE OF
KNIVES TO YOU,
TO CUT THE THREAD
OF LOVE IF 'T NOT TRUE.**

—SIXTEENTH CENTURY POEM

Knives and gloves were popular wedding presents in sixteenth-century England, and brides wore both with their wedding finery.

When Mark Antony
and Cleopatra became
lovers, he gave her Phoenicia,
Coele-Syria, Cyprus, and
part of Cilicia, Arabia,
and Judea.

"'Twas the night before Christmas,
when all through the house..."
Clement C. Moore wrote this poem in
1822 and gave it to his children
as a Christmas gift.

LOVE SOUGHT IS GOOD, BUT GIVEN UNSOUGHT IS BETTER.

—Shakespeare

BOOKS TO READ WHEN YOUR LOVER HAS GONE

Contributed by librarians across the U.S.

	The Bible
H. Halpern, Ph.D.	**How to Break Your Addiction to a Person**
S. Keen, Ph.D.	**What to Do When You're Bored and Blue**
L. Buscaglia	**Living, Loving and Learning**
M. Yates	**Coping: A Survival Manual for Women Alone**
G. Sheehy	**Passages**

—Dolores Ramsey et al., Wichita Public Library, Wichita, Kansas

S. Maugham	**Of Human Bondage**
N. Ephron	**Heartburn**
L. Tolstoy	**Anna Karenina**

—Johanna Zea et al., San Francisco Public Library, San Francisco, California

H. Miller	**Tropic of Cancer**
E. Jong	**Fear of Flying**
J. Kerouac	**The Subterraneans**
Wallerstein	**Surviving the Breakup**
J. Epstein	**Divorced in America**

—Patrick Fiore et al., Brooklyn Public Library, Brooklyn, New York

Dear John,

If the reason is another love,
a breakdown in trust or the loss
of feelings, the person who is to be left
has a right to know. It takes time,
but in most cases it's easier,
with time, to deal with the truth.

—Cheryl Merser,
Honorable Intentions

It ain't over till i
—Yogi Berra

The opposite of love isn't
hate. It's indifference.
—Anonymous

I never hated a man enough
to give his diamonds back.
—Zsa Zsa Gabor

Jealousy is not a sign of insecurity or of competitiveness
alone—but of love, according to Dr. Sidney Lecker.
You wouldn't be afraid of losing someone or even want to
compete for their affections unless you loved them, he reasons.
Lecker, director of Behavior Science for the Executive
Health Examiners Group, made his remarks several years
ago on a WNBC-TV program about love.
What's more, Lecker disagrees with a widespread belief that
something is wrong with your relationship if you have to ask your
mate if he or she loves you. "Many spouses feel rejected
when they have to ask for love," he said, "so they stop giving
it." This can often be the beginning of the end of the
relationship unless the misunderstanding is cleared up.

The man who is not jealous
in love, does not love.
—Berber proverb

Jealousy is the great exaggerator.
—Schiller

over.

The world's biggest hug was hugged on August 10, 1980, when an estimated 24,000 people linked arms around the USC campus in Los Angeles. The hug opened that year's International Marriage Encounter convention.

A German scientist says that a man's pulse rate increases from 72 to 110 when he kisses, and a woman's increases to 108.

Ways to say "kiss": Peck, buss, mash, osculation, smack, smooch, first base.

Ten most huggable people in the world, according to the International Hug Center, Pittsburgh:

1. Pope John Paul II
2. Lech Walesa
3. E.T.
4. George Burns
5. Alan Alda
6. Betty Ford
7. Ruth Gordon
8. Coretta King
9. Jimmy Stewart
10. Leo Buscaglia

Different kinds of kisses: 💋 your money goodbye, 💋 mah grits, give someone the 💋-off, get the 💋-off, 💋 the dust (die), 💋 the canvas (get knocked down in boxing), 💋ing cousins, chocolate 💋es, 💋 of death, and butterfly 💋 (batting your eyelashes against someone's cheek).

Debbie Luray and Jim Schuyler of Florida kissed for five days The kiss went on record as

Who is Leo Buscaglia?
a) Italian tenor who sang "Be My Love."
b) Professor who taught Love 1A at USC.
c) Organizer of Valentine's Day parade in St. Regis Falls, New York.
d) Lyricist who wrote "Love Potion #9."

Answer: *b* He's the bestselling author of eight books about love and life. He's also champion of hugging and its positive physiological effects on people. His Love 1A course was one of the most popular at USC.

The lower you kissed a person in the Middle Ages, the higher your respect. You kissed someone important on the hand, someone even more important on the hem, and for a true bigshot you kissed the ground.

An archeologist and teacher at Texas A & M University believes that the custom of kissing was first introduced by Eastern Indians 4,000 years ago. Their writings contain references to people pressing noses together. For more info, you can take the course at A & M called "The Origin of Kissing."

In love, there is always one who kisses and one who offers the cheek.
—French proverb

and twelve hours for a Valentine's Day charity event in 1980. being one of history's longest.

Since tennis originated in medieval France, scholars theorize that the scoring term "love" came from the French word for egg—*l'oeuf*—and implied, as we say now, "a big fat goose egg," or nothing. The word "tennis" comes from the French *tenez*, which means "attention."

The cognitive-affective state characterized by intrusive and obsessive fantasizing concerning reciprocity of amorant feeling by the object of the amorance, or OA.
—The definition of being in love offered by a delegate at the first International Conference on Love and Attraction in 1977.

If you're not getting anywhere using the same old words to describe your amorous feelings, try these substitutes from *Roget's Thesaurus*:
love: shine up to, pitch woo, spoon, set one's cap for
beautiful: well-composed, well-grouped, undeformed, undefaced, unspotted
passion: predilection
amorous: amative
care: probity, vigil

BABABADALGH-ARAGHTALKAM-MINARRONNK-ONNBRONNYTO-NNERRONNTU-ONNTHUNNTR-OVARRHOUNA-WNSKAWNTOO-HOOHOORENE-NTHURNUK.

—Word symbolizing fall of Adam and Eve in *Finnegans Wake*, by James Joyce

A Chinese journalist studying communication at Stanford University wrote an article about U.S. singles' bars and commented that "sexy" is medical jargon in China. "No one thinks of it as a compliment," she said. "I can't imagine what kind of face my boyfriend in Beijing would make if I told him I thought he was 'sexy.'"

The Chinese word that approximates our definition of sexy translates as *sex-feeling* in English but the word is used only when speaking of females.

POSSLQ
—Anacronym coined by the U.S. Census Bureau for "persons of the opposite sex sharing living quarters."

—Harpo Marx

And do as adversaries
do in law,
Strive mightily, but eat and
drink as friends.
—Shakespeare

In California, a married person who quits a job to follow a spouse to a new location is entitled to unemployment compensation. A few years ago a county court ruled that unmarried lovers were also entitled to these benefits.

But in June 1983, the California Supreme Court overturned the ruling, saying that to rule the other way would place a burden on administrative agencies to "ferret out the 'true depth' and intimacy of a relationship in order to determine whether the existence and nature of the relationship was the equivalent of marriage."

While the United States was at war in 1941, a Georgia lawyer used a little-known law to get his client a divorce from her husband. The law, enacted during the Civil War when Georgia and the United States were on opposite sides, provided grounds for divorce if the spouse was "in the military service of the United States."

---

3 things I love besides law as told by Melvin Belli:
1. Television
   2. Traveling
      3. Outer space movies

Susan Liptrot is suing an ex-lover because:
a) She says he gave her herpes.
b) He promised to love her always but stopped.
c) He married her while still married to someone else.
d) He sawed her house in half.

Answer: a Liptrot says he neglected to tell her of his herpes before they had sex. She hopes the case will "help people be more informed about herpes and take more sexual responsibility."

Several years ago Tom Hansen of Boulder, Colorado, sued his parents for "psychological malparenting" and claimed $350,000 in damages. Hansen, then 24, said he chose to sue instead of acting on a desire to kill his father.

He lost the case and appealed. In December 1979, the court of appeals upheld the initial judgment, ruling in favor of his parents.

In January 1955, Fanny Ennis, 69, brought suit against John Purser, 73, in Ockley, England, for breach of promise. She said he'd promised to marry her in 1908 and still hadn't.

Ralph agrees not to pick, nag, or comment about Wanda's skin blemishes.
—Clause in a marriage contract, as reported by *Time* magazine

"do."

Poet Elizabeth Barrett was an invalid confined to her house by her tyrannical father when Robert Browning, another poet, initiated contact with Elizabeth through a letter which ended, "I love your works, my dear Miss Barrett, and I love you too."

The two corresponded passionately and met face-to-face in the spring of 1845. Elizabeth's health improved immensely, they eloped, and moved to Italy, where they lived for fifteen years.

During their first few years together, Elizabeth—or Ba, or "my little Portuguese," as Robert sometimes called her—worked secretly on a manuscript of poems. One morning, as David Loth tells it in *The Brownings: A Victorian Idyll*, "she thrust something bulky into his pocket. Before he could turn she had fled from the room. . . . Page after page he read . . . the sonnets poured out for him the crescendo of passion that reached its climax with, 'How do I love thee? Let me count the ways. . . ,' "

The collection of sonnets, which Browning termed "the finest written in any language since Shakespeare's," was published under the title *Sonnets from the Portuguese*. Elizabeth died in Robert's arms in June 1861, at the age of 54, of tuberculosis.

The letters which chronicled the early years of the Brownings' romance were sold at public auction in 1937 for $15,000.

*She loved the writer before
she knew the man.*

When men and women are in love and reading a love
letter, they read for all they are worth. They read every
word three ways; they read between the lines and in
the margins...they may even take the punctuation
into account. Then, if never before or after, they read.
—Mortimer J. Adler, quoted in *Quote*

Dear You,

*you are a wretch, truly perverse,
truly stupid, a real Cinderella*

Who penned these words in a letter,
and to whom?
a) John Hinckley to Jodie Foster
b) Napoleon to Josephine
c) Richard Burton to Liz Taylor
d) King Henry VIII to Anne Boleyn
Answer: b

—Western Union Standard Telegram,
circa 1969

```
742P PST FEB 14 69 LO134
L SO 540 BL PDF SAN JOSE CALIF 17 533 PPST
MR PAUL SINN
   465 SOUTH FIFTH ST APT D SAN JOSE CALIF
I LIKE YOU I LOVE YOU I WANT YOU ALL THE TIME
SO PLEASE WIRE ME BACK THAT YOU'LL BE MY VALENTINE
```

In England, people send their valentines
to the town of Lover to be postmarked.
After hand-stamping 1,400 valentines in 1981,
Lover postal clerk Lucy Southorn said,
"It made my arm ache a bit."

dear John,

A Taiwanese man wrote 700 love letters to his girlfriend over a two-year period in hopes that she would marry him. According to a Taiwan newspaper, the woman did get married—to the postman who delivered all the letters.

Happy Valentine's Day.

For this was Seynt Valentine's day. When every foul cometh ther to choose his mate. —Chaucer

No one really knows how an early martyr named Valentine, who met a grisly death, came to be associated with the exchanging of cards on the day bearing his name. One theory is that in Europe during the Middle Ages birds began to mate on February 14.

During the Middle Ages, people who couldn't write would sign a contract with an X and kiss it to show sincerity. That's how X's at the bottom of letters came to symbolize kisses.

love + xxx

How to write a

For the first thirty pages, set your scene and characters. On page thirty-one, the hero will say "Good morning." For the next ten pages, the heroine will wonder what he meant by that.
—The late Peggy Roth, romance novel editor, on the formula for writing a Gothic romance. Quoted by Yvonne MacManus in her bestselling book *You Can Write a Romance! And Get It Published!*

More than seventy new romance novels appear in bookstores each month. That's forty percent of all paperbacks sold and $350 million in 1983 alone. You, too, can become a Brandy LaRue or a Barbara Cartland even if your name is John Smith.

Three steps to stardom:

♥ **1. Read, read, read the romances already out there,** say the experts, and decide which type you feel most comfortable with. Each has a unique formula. Briefly:

Category romance. Short and sweet, currently the best selling. Woman meets irresistible man, hearts throb, sparks fly, but a misunderstanding tears them apart. She broods, a coincidence brings them back together, they resolve the conflict and make a commitment. Sex usually doesn't progress beyond foreplay unless there's commitment.

Historical romance. Also called "bodice rippers." Set in any period before World War I. *Gone With the Wind* is the most famous example. Often very long.

Contemporary romance. Medium length, about a woman with modern problems; for example, she meets a man who dies, then meets another man, who also dies.

Teen romance. Heroine is fifteen or sixteen, blossoms when she meets boy. Sexual desire stirs, but as one editor puts it, "Our characters will not follow through on their desire." Confusion always evolves into caring.

Regency romance. Set during the Regency period (early 1800's) in England. Reads like a light Jane Austen novel. No sex.

Suspense/Gothic romance. Any of the above set in a gloomy mansion with creaky stairs and plot twists.

♥ **2. Choose a pen name.** The prettier, the better. Those already taken include Jennifer Wilde, Vanessa Royall, Megan Barker, Alicia Grace, and Fortune Kent—and these are for male authors.

Remember that last names beginning with "A" will be too high on the shelf to catch browsers' attention while those beginning with "Z" will be too low.

♥ **3. Get in the mood.** Many romance writers use gimmicks to get started on their purple prose. Parris Afton Bonds wears a negligee. Bertrice Small stares at a Tom Selleck poster. And Danielle Steel munches on heart-shaped toast and caviar.

When writing breathy passages try to go beyond the Pillaging Mouth. Vivian Stephens, romance writer, offered this advice at a recent romance writers' seminar: "I am really tired of nipples. You must *diversify*. You must go to areas of the body other than those that are commonly known!"

Recommended reading: *How to Write a Romance and Get It Published*, K. Falk; *How to Write Romance Novels That Sell*, M. Lowery; *You Can Write a Romance! And Get It Published!* Y. MacManus.

2 ROMANTIC ANECDOTES ABOUT ERNEST HEMINGWAY.

As told for The Book of Love by Juanita Jensen, Hemingway's Secretary in Cuba form 1949-1952.

1.   We were spending a weekend on Ernest's fishing boat, <u>Pilar.</u> We had anchored in the most beautiful lagoon and I swam ashore with a friend. The water was crystal clear and we could see every pebble on the bottom. We were only on the beach a few minutes when Gregorio, who ran the boat and was Ernest's cheff cook, called us to come back for lunch. We waded into the water to swim back, and there was a huge shark swimming back and forth, right between us and the boat.

There was no way I was going into that water so I yelled for Ernest. When he saw what was going on, he took off his glasses, put a knife between his teeth, and dove in. He accompanied us back to the boat. I don't think I've ever swam that fast.

Afterwards, Gregorio told me it was just a cat shark and that he was probably more afraid of us than we were of him. But Papa was so sympathetic and maybe even a little disappointed that he didn't get to use the knife or fight the shark.

*   *   *

2.   When I told Ernest I was going to be married
he offered to give us a reception at the Finca. I
asked him if he would give me away and he accepted,
but every few days before the wedding he would ask
his wife, Mary, [Hemingway's wife] if it was absolutely necessary for
him to wear socks. She said of course, and that he
was to wear his suit. But he never quite gave up.
He kept hoping right up till the last minute that Mary
would say he didn't have to wear socks.

    But socks he wore. I think he was relieved
when it was over so he could get back to the Finca with
no socks and his loafers. When we arrived there for the
reception, he and Don Andres, a Basque priest friend
of his, were busy shooting off a miniature cannon
Ernest had, making a noise you could hear all through
town. They were doing it with such glee, like a couple
of little boys.

                    *   *   *

And then I asked him with my eyes
to ask again yes and then he asked me would I
yes to say yes my mountain flower and first
I put my arms around him yes and drew him
down to me so he could feel my breasts
all perfume yes and his heart was going
like mad and yes
I said yes
I will,

—James Joyce, *Ulysses*

A. A. Milne's books *When We Were Very Young* and *Now We Are Six* were written in the 1920's for and about the author's son, Christopher Robin. *Winnie-the-Pooh* and *The House at Pooh Corner* chronicled the adventures of Pooh, Christopher's teddy bear. Today, the real Christopher Robin Milne is in his sixties and lives in Devon, England.

A school teacher and a farmer met each other at their local library in Idaho. When the pair got married several years ago, they held the ceremony at the library.

What was the original title of the book *Lady Chatterley's Lover*?
a) *The Gardener and the Lady*
b) *Tiptoe Through the Tulips*
c) *Splendor in the Grass*
d) *Tenderness*

Answer: d

Write a Love Poem Fortnight begins on April 23 every year, on what is believed to be the birthdate of William Shakespeare (no one knows Will's birth date for certain). The event is sponsored by the Unicorn Hunters of Lake Superior College, Michigan, "to encourage you to write a poem to the loved one of your choice."

For never was a story of more woe than this of Juliet and her Romeo.
—Shakespeare
Experts believe Shakespeare's story of the star-crossed lovers is fictional and based on a novel by Luigi da Porto published in 1529.

Cinderella lost a glass slipper because a translator goofed. The story originally involved a fur-lined slipper, but the English translator took the French word *vair* to mean "glass" (*verre*) instead of "fur."

Ba! Ba! Black Sheep was one of the original titles of which book?
a) *The Farmer's Daughter*
b) *Gone With the Wind*
c) *Uncle Tom's Cabin*
d) *Love Story*

Answer: b

Giovanni Casanova (1725–1798) reportedly seduced thousands of women and spent the last years of his life as a librarian.

How do I love thee? Let me count the ways.
—Elizabeth Barrett Browning, in a sonnet for Robert Browning. The two met and fell in love through letters. (See *Love & Letters*.)

LUCKY IN CARDS, UNLUCKY IN LO♥E.

—Proverb

According to the Polish newspaper *Vecerny Pravda*, Vera Czermak jumped out of her third-story window when she learned her husband was two-timing her. Mrs. Czermak recovered in the hospital after landing on her husband, who was ki__ed.

OOPS

In China,
marriage certificates
are printed on
red paper,
the traditional
Chinese color for
good luck.
On the back of each
certificate
is stamped the
message,

"Practice thrift, frugality and birth control."

LOVE IS LOVELIER THE 2ND TIME AROUND

Albertine and Layman Musser were married on August 24, 1918. They got divorced in 1932, and each married some-one else. Forty-nine years later in 1981, both widowed, they met again. The two renewed their courtship and re-married—on the same date, and with the same rings. "I longed for the smell of the lotion he used," she says now. Her advice? "Don't be too proud to fight for your love."

After a decade of decline in the state of marriage, the United States is experiencing a wedding boom. Not coincidentally, there's been a decline in the divorce rate over the last few years.

Man with most wives: King Mongkut, Siam (1804–1868), 9,000 wives and concubines. He was the king in *The King and I*. Woman with most hus-bands: Queen Kahena, Barbary, 400 husbands.

To marry for a first time is to begin again as oneself. To marry again is to begin again, again.
—David Thomson, *Film Comment*

TO HAVE AND TO HOLD FROM THIS DAY FORWARD, FOR BETTER, FOR WORSE, FOR RICHER, FOR POORER, IN SICKNESS, AND IN HEALTH, TO LOVE AND TO CHERISH, TILL DEATH DO US PART.
—Book of Common Prayer

A Middle Tennessee State University study shows that men and women want the same qualities in a mate: dependabil-ity and mutual attraction.

The survey results were compared with answers given to the same questions in a survey forty-five years ago. Cooking and cleaning skills, placed high on the list of desirables by men back then, ranked at the bottom half this time.

The study also asked what men *think* women want, and vice versa. Says psychology professor W. Beryl West, who led the Middle Tennessee research team: "Men still believe they must bear the brunt of the financial burden…and women still feel they should cook dinner after a hard day at work."

It is therefore our glorious and divine purpose to fly mountains, to sow petal-scent...to glorify glory, to love with love.
Thank you for choosing an outrageous cuss like me.
This is the purest double helix of our us-ness.
—A sampling of do-it-yourself wedding vows as reported in *Time* magazine.

Our mistake was getting married the second time.
—Elizabeth Taylor about Richard Burton, on ABC's *Good Morning America*.

ELIZABETH
~~TAYLOR~~
~~HILTON~~
~~WILDING~~
~~TODD~~
~~FISHER~~
~~BURTON~~
~~BURTON~~
~~WARNER~~

"DO YOU? I DO."
"DO I? I DO."

Q. What's black and white and gold, costs nothing, and entitles you (or anyone) to perform weddings?
A. A ministry certificate from Universal Life Church.

Hundreds of thousands of couples have been legally married by friends ordained by mail through ULC. It's ideal if you want to design your own ceremony, write your own vows, or just be different.

To become a minister, send a letter requesting ordination to Universal Life Church, 601 Third Street, Modesto, CA 95351. Sign the certificate they send you, register your name and address with the church, and you're ordained. According to ULC Reverend Rex Ames, you may perform weddings or be married by a ULC minister anywhere in the United States (though we suggest you check local laws). Ordination costs nothing but the church does appreciate "good-will" donations. That's how it has stayed afloat for twenty years and it seems to be doing fine; founder Kirby James Hensley once told *Newsweek* that "it has all been profitable beyond my dreams."

If you won't settle for being (or being married by) a minister, the church will gladly bestow other titles. Among the choices: Reverend Mother, Lama, Guru, Archdeacon, Abbot, Monsignor, Brahman. For an extra five dollars, ULC will even ordain you as a saint.

Recommended reading for writing your own vows: *The New Wedding*, K. Arisian; *Write Your Own Wedding*, M. Brill et al.

WHAT TO DO IF YOU WANT TO MARRY MORE THAN ONE PERSON

If you are a man you can practice *polygyny*—marriage of a man to more than one woman. A woman can practice *polyandry*—marriage of a woman to more than one man. *Polygamy* refers to any multiple marriage.

Polygamous marriages have been abolished throughout most parts of the world, but there are exceptions. Here's how you might capitalize on them:

Become a Mormon. It has been estimated that as many as 30,000 Mormons in the United States practice polygyny secretly.

Get rich and move to Hong Kong. Polygyny is not unusual in Hong Kong, especially among wealthy men able to support more than one wife. "You get tired of one woman and want to marry another," confides a resident.

Move to Subsaharan Africa. In Subsaharan Africa and in some Eastern Muslim societies, wives welcome the addition of other wives to the family because it means less work.

Take up farming in Tibet. A woman can have more than one husband in Tibet, though this is not as glamorous as it may sound. Brothers of the same family share the same wife so that farms, already small in that country, can be passed down through generations without being broken up.

In Japan, bride and groom seal their union with three sips of sake.

Love is a bonus, not a must.
—Japanese bride, 1981

One of the most expensive weddings in history took place on June 16, 1979, between Maria Niarchos, then 20, and Alix Chevassus, then 36. Guests drank an estimated 12,000 bottles of champagne and red wine. Total tab for the affair exceeded $500,000.

Which store claims to sell more wedding gowns than any other?
a) Macy's, San Francisco
b) Neiman-Marcus, Dallas
c) Salvation Army, Los Angeles
d) Bergdorf Goodman, New York

Answer: c

I do. I do. I do.
I do. I do. I do.
I do. I do. I do.
I do. I do. I do.
I do. I do. I do.

Jack and Edna Moran of Seattle were married for the first time on July 27, 1937, and forty times since then—all to each other. They are history's most married couple.

In Japan, a marriage arranged by a woman's family, friends, boss, or wedding service is the norm. High on the list of preferences for a husband is coming home early. Other considerations are the groom's university background, looks, and whether he is employed by a company listed on the Tokyo Stock Exchange.

Anthropologist Margaret Mead advocated a two-step marriage. In the first step, the couple would agree to live together but not have any children. Legally, the relationship could be ended whenever the couple chose.
   The second step would be undertaken when the couple decided to have children. They would have to show they could support the children they intended to have, and would be required to make a lifetime commitment.
   Mead was married three times and wrote about the relationships in her critically acclaimed autobiography, *Blackberry Winter*.

It is better to love two too many, than one too few.
—Sir John Harington, *Epigrams*

HOW TO GET MARRIED FAST

Nevada is still the place to be married almost as fast as you can say "I do." Of all states, it's the only one that requires neither blood test nor waiting period.

In Las Vegas, the courthouse is open weekdays from eight A.M. to midnight, weekends and holidays twenty-four hours a day. Cost for a license is twenty-five dollars, cash or traveler's checks. A civil ceremony can be performed at the courthouse for twenty-five dollars during regular business hours, thirty dollars after. Or you can opt for a wedding in a Las Vegas wedding chapel. Examples:

Chapel of the Stars. "Your wedding will be as beautiful as the moment you first fell in love," says the ad in the yellow pages. Hostess Juanita Brown thinks the chapel's beauty is what sets it apart. Most unusual wedding: "A Halloween wedding. They wanted dead flowers and we had to get 'em out of the garbage can. That was hard."

Cupid's Wedding Chapel. "We take care of our people," stresses manager Betty Parry. Cupid's does weddings to go, and recently arranged one at the bottom of Hoover Dam, "in the elevator where the couple first met." Most unusual wedding: "It's three A.M. and you go to the door and they've all got guns. They want a handgun wedding." Parry said the groom demonstrates gunfights in Arizona for a living and requested "something out of the ordinary." The best man held a gun to the groom while he said the vows.

Circus Circus Chapel of the Fountain. "We've got our ministers and photographers on beepers. And our decor is outstanding," says manager Marjorie Workhoven. There's a wedding photograph of Liz Taylor and Eddie Fisher in the chapel lobby, but no one is sure if that means they got married there, or what. Most unusual wedding: a couple dressed as Rhett Butler and Scarlett O'Hara. Scarlett's dress had huge hoops, "which made it hard to get through the casino between the slot machines," says Workhoven. See *Love & Animals* for another of Marjorie's unusual weddings.

We've Only Just Begun Wedding Chapel. There are two branches in Las Vegas, both run by Charlotte Richards, the grande dame of Las Vegas wedding chapels. She's done four of Mickey Rooney's eight weddings. "During number seven, four of his ex-wives sat in the first pew," she says. They make every wedding special, and they don't rush people through, according to Richards. Most unusual wedding: a couple whose ceremony was interrupted when the bride-to-be rushed off to have her baby. "They came back two weeks later and completed the ceremony."

♥ **If this doesn't work out, turn the page**

HOW TO GET DIVORCED FAST

While there are about thirty wedding chapels in Las Vegas, there are more than sixty firms there willing to help you arrange a divorce—all listed in the yellow pages after the classification for "Ditching Services."

A Nevada divorce can be over and done with in twenty-four hours providing you've fulfilled the six-week residency requirement.

Depending on laws in your state or country, a faster alternative might be Haiti. There, too, you can get a divorce in twenty-four hours and there's no residency requirement. Do check local laws, though, because you might find that a Haiti-style divorce is not recognized where you live.

Haiti has another advantage: You can combine your divorce—or soften its unpleasantry, perhaps—with a vacation. At least, that's the mood imparted by Fresh Pond Travel Tours of Natick, Massachusetts, "largest tour operator of divorce packages in the Caribbean." The quickie divorce tours are a sideline for the travel agency and are the result of a travel agent married to an attorney, according to travel agent half Diane Whitsitt.

Total cost for a Haitian divorce through FP Tours is $450, excluding airfare.

And when it's all taken care of, says their brochure, "plaintiff or defendant may remarry the day after the appearance in Court." FP will make all arrangements for remarriage, the cost for which is $100.

Divorce laws in China have eased somewhat in recent years and the divorce rate has shot up. The Chinese bureau which studies such statistics attributes this rise mostly to "fickleness which can be caused by gold-digging, social climbing, and unsatisfied sexual desire."

DIVORCE VENDING-MACHINE STYLE

In the non-Mormon town of Corinne, Utah, in the 1870's, people could get quickie divorces from a vending machine for $2.50. Such divorces were eventually ruled illegal, making bigamists of those who had gotten one and remarried.

No one took much notice, though, because bigamy in Utah among Mormons was common then.

THOSE CRAZY DIVORCE LAWS

Or, just because you're crazy in California doesn't mean you're crazy in Idaho—not enough to get divorced, anyway.

Insanity is grounds for divorce in twenty-two states, though the length of time you or your spouse must be insane varies from state to state. In some cases, *how* insane you must be also varies. To wit:

Utah: Permanently insane
Colorado: Incurably insane
Wisconsin: Insane for one year
Alaska: Insane for eighteen months
Georgia, Hawaii, Indiana, Nevada, New Jersey, Oregon, Washington, Wyoming: Insane for two years
Arkansas, California, Florida, Maryland, Minnesota, Mississippi, North Carolina, Texas, West Virginia: Insane for three years
Idaho: Insane for six years
Kansas: Incompatibility by reason of insanity or incapacity
(Compiled from the 1983 *World Almanac*.)

MORE TRUTH THAN FICTION TO SEVEN-YEAR ITCH

The 1980 Census determined that the median duration of American marriages is 6.8 years. Half of all marriages last that long, and half last longer. The bulk of divorces are obtained between the second and seventh anniversary.

YOU WANT TO PUT WHAT ON MY WHAT?

Anna Swick of Pittsburgh got a divorce in April 1951 on the grounds that her husband "was always trying to tattoo me so he could open a circus."

♥San Diego sex therapist Dr. Theresa Crenshaw saw a correlation between sexual well-being and the economy when interest rates fluctuated wildly.

"Every time interest rates went over eighteen percent," she told *San Diego* magazine, "droves of impotent men came to see me."

She said she could tell how many patients she would have on a given day, and what their problems would be, just by reading the morning paper.

For more about Dr. Crenshaw, also see *Love & Aphrodisiacs* and *Love & Sex*.

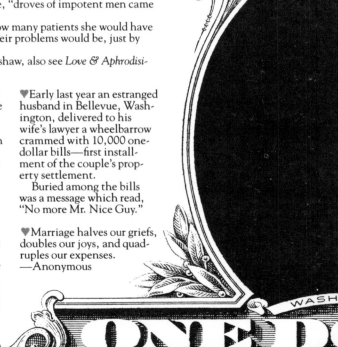

♥"Familial Love and Intertemporal Optimality" is the name of a paper by Brown University professor Herschel I. Grossman on which subject?
a) Effects of family love on family finances.
b) How much family love costs the average taxpayer.
c) Psychological adjustment of families who pay more than $100 a year to frequent family-type nudist camps.
d) The rising cost of family therapy.

Answer: a See *Love & Science* for Grossman's equation which explains it all.

♥Early last year an estranged husband in Bellevue, Washington, delivered to his wife's lawyer a wheelbarrow crammed with 10,000 one-dollar bills—first installment of the couple's property settlement.

Buried among the bills was a message which read, "No more Mr. Nice Guy."

♥Marriage halves our griefs, doubles our joys, and quadruples our expenses.
—Anonymous

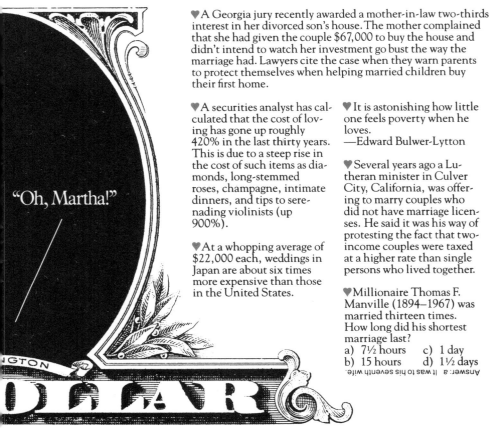

"Oh, Martha!"

♥ A Georgia jury recently awarded a mother-in-law two-thirds interest in her divorced son's house. The mother complained that she had given the couple $67,000 to buy the house and didn't intend to watch her investment go bust the way the marriage had. Lawyers cite the case when they warn parents to protect themselves when helping married children buy their first home.

♥ A securities analyst has calculated that the cost of loving has gone up roughly 420% in the last thirty years. This is due to a steep rise in the cost of such items as diamonds, long-stemmed roses, champagne, intimate dinners, and tips to serenading violinists (up 900%).

♥ At a whopping average of $22,000 each, weddings in Japan are about six times more expensive than those in the United States.

♥ It is astonishing how little one feels poverty when he loves.
—Edward Bulwer-Lytton

♥ Several years ago a Lutheran minister in Culver City, California, was offering to marry couples who did not have marriage licenses. He said it was his way of protesting the fact that two-income couples were taxed at a higher rate than single persons who lived together.

♥ Millionaire Thomas F. Manville (1894–1967) was married thirteen times. How long did his shortest marriage last?
a) 7½ hours   c) 1 day
b) 15 hours   d) 1½ days

Answer: a. It was to his seventh wife.

21 POPULAR LOVE SONGS THAT ASK QUESTIONS

1. "Are You Mine?"
2. "Are You Really Mine?"
3. "Are You Sure?"
4. "Are You Teasing Me?"
5. "Are You Sincere?"
6. "How Can I Replace You?"
7. "How Could You Believe Me When I Said I Love You When You Know I've Been a Liar All My Life?"
8. "Somebody Bad Stole de Wedding Bell (Who's Got de Ding Dong?)"
9. "What Kind of Fool Am I?"
10. "What Kind of Fool Do You Think I Am?"
11. "Where Were You On Our Wedding Day?"
12. "Where, Oh Where?"
13. "Who Knows?"
14. "Who Put The Bomp (In the Bomp Ba Bomp Ba Bomp)"
15. "(Why Did I Tell You I Was Going to) Shanghai"
16. "Why Do Fools Fall In Love?"
17. "Why Don't You Believe Me?"
18. "Why Don't You Love Me?"
19. "Why Don't You Write Me?"
20. "Why Why?"
21. "Why Baby Why?"

A Düsseldorf, Germany, engineer got a divorce in 1983 on the grounds that his wife "listened to music or played the piano from morning to night."

"When I wanted to make love to Helga," he said, "Richard Wagner was glaring at me from the wall opposite our bed. She should have married Mozart."

♪

After violinist Itzhak Perlman played at a July Fourth concert, Toby Friedlander —then a stranger—rushed backstage and said, "Will you marry me?" He accepted four years later and they were married in 1967.

♪

I love, you love, we all love, why do we love, who do we love, how much do we love, where do we love, why did you stop loving me?
—Mitch Miller, on the theme of love in popular songs.

♪

Love you madly.
—Duke Ellington to his audiences.

10 SONGS TO PLAY ON THE FIRST DATE

1. "Ooh Baby Baby" (Robinson-Moore)—**The Miracles**
2. "If I Fell" (Lennon-McCartney)—**The Beatles**
3. "Betcha by Golly, Wow" (Bell-Creed)—**The Stylistics**
4. "You Send Me" (Cooke)—**Sam Cooke**
5. "In the Midnight Hour" (Pickett-Cropper)—**Wilson Pickett**

6. "Good Vibrations" (Wilson-Love)—**The Beach Boys**
7. "Just One Look" (Carroll-Payne)—**Doris Troy**
8. "I Can't Help Myself" (Holland-Dozier-Holland)—**The Four Tops**
9. "I Want to Hold Your Hand" (Lennon-McCartney)—**The Beatles**
10. "You Really Got Me" (Davies)—**The Kinks**

—Brant Mewborn, singer/songwriter and editor and writer, *Rolling Stone* magazine.

10 SONGS TO AVOID ON THE FIRST DATE.

1. "...Why Don't We Do It in the Road?" (Lennon-McCartney) —The Beatles

2. "Sex Machine" (Brown-Byrd-Lennhoff) —James Brown

3. "Love Stinks" (Wolf-Justman) —J. Geils Band

4. "Don't Stand So Close to Me" (Sting) —The Police

5. "(I Can't Get No) Satisfaction" (Jagger-Richards) —The Rolling Stones

6. "Psycho Killer" (Byrne-Weymouth-Frantz) —Talking Heads

7. "You're No Good" (Ballard) —Linda Ronstadt

8. "Tainted Love" (Cobb) —Soft Cell

9. "Anarchy in the U.K." (Cook-Jones-Matlock-Rotten) —The Sex Pistols

10. "Strangers in the Night" (Singleton-Snyder-Kaempfert) —Frank Sinatra

—Brant Mewborn, singer/songwriter and editor and writer, *Rolling Stone* magazine.

They're Playing Our Song had its world premiere in Los Angeles December 1, 1978. This Neil Simon play was based on a relationship sparked by a collaboration between lyricist Carole Bayer Sager and musician Marvin Hamlisch—who together wrote the words and music for the songs in the play.

♫

We were singing "All You Need Is Love"...but love is just a gift, and it doesn't answer everything and it's like a precious plant that you have to nurture and look after and all that.
—John Lennon, quoted in *The Ballad of John and Yoko*

♫

It is as absurd to say that a man can't love one woman all the time as it is to say that a violinist needs several violins to play the same piece of music.
—Honoré de Balzac

All of me.
—Song title, Seymour Simons and Gerald Marks.

We are one.
—Slogan for the Woodstock Music Festival, which commenced August 15, 1969, on a farm in New York, lasted three days, and drew a crowd of almost half a million people.

♫

People about whom love songs have been sung: Billie Jean, Billy Joe, G-L-O-R-I-A, Lisa/Julie, Louie Louie, Mary, Diana, Donna, Venus, Michelle, Peggy Sue, Barbara Ann, Wendy, Patricia, Lola, Suzie-Q, Maryanne.

♫

Neil Sedaka sang the song, "Breaking Up Is Hard to Do" in the mid-1970's. Who sang the version which was popular in the early 1960's?
a) Ruby and the Romantics
b) Barbara Lewis
c) Neil Sedaka
d) Chubby Checker

Where love can be found, according to songwriters:
On the back porch, on the rocks, on top of the world, standing there, down by the old mill stream, just around the corner, across a crowded room, under my skin, under my thumb, back in New England, between the moon and New York City, under the boardwalk, under the apple tree, ridin' in your car, on the street where you live, three times on the ceiling, up where we belong, inside of me, and with the one you're with.

♫

I kissed my first woman and smoked my first cigarette on the same day. I have never had time for tobacco since.
—Arturo Toscanini

♫

The world's all-time best-selling love song, according to the *Guinness Book of World Records*: "Let Me Call You Sweetheart."

Answer: c

July 29, 1981, was the day Prince Charles and Princess Diana were married. It was also the day a mysterious new flower bloomed at the Waimea Arboretum and Botanical Garden in Hawaii. ♥
The white beauty turned out to be a hybrid of two different varieties of hibiscus from separate islands, and no one knows how they got together. The bloom was named "Royal Wedding." Cuttings were forwarded to the Royal Botanical Gardens in London. ♥
As Scandinavian mythology has it, the good god of light was killed by the bad god with a mistletoe dart. It became a custom to kiss under the mistletoe to show that the plant was no longer a symbol of death, but of love. It's bad luck to say no to someone who wants to kiss you under the mistletoe. ♥
Friendship is a plant of slow growth, and must undergo and withstand the shocks of adversity before it is entitled to the appellation.
—George Washington

♥ 4 UNUSUAL REQUESTS FOR WEDDING FLOWERS AND GREENERY FROM FLOWER FASHIONS, INC., BEVERLY HILLS

1. Karen Black's 1975 sunrise wedding-in-the-woods. The Flower Fashions crew was up most of the night at the Beverly Hills reservoir clearing land and tying ribbons and flower garlands onto trees.

2. A nudist wedding in which the bride carried a small nosegay. "I don't think the groom wore a boutonniere," says co-owner Fred Gibbons.

3. Fifth Dimension singer Florence LaRue's wedding in a hot air balloon festooned with flowers.

4. A winter-theme wedding in the heat of a Las Vegas summer for a casino owner's daughter. Flower Fashions flew in fresh evergreens and created frozen fountains and two ice skating rinks. The bridesmaids wore fur.

♥ Nobody loves me. I'm going into the garden and eat worms.
—Anonymous

It's been said that Lincoln was to be married on January 1, 1841, but didn't show up for the wedding. Almost two years later, however, he married Mary Todd (same woman) on the spur of the moment.

If we cannot end now our differences, at least we can help make the world safe for diversity.
—John F. Kennedy

The happiest moments of my life have been the few which I have passed at home in the bosom of my family.
—Thomas Jefferson

Lots and lots of love. Kiss the baby.
—Harry Truman, closing of his letters to his wife Bess.

History has it that George Washington fell in love with Sally Fairfax, his best friend's wife, during a six-month stay at Mount Vernon in 1755.

Letters to Sally reveal Washington's passion, but there is no evidence he ever acted on his feelings. In 1759 he married Martha Dandridge Custis.

Carrie darling sweetheart adorable,
—Warren G. Harding, salutation of his love letters to Mrs. Carrie Phillips.

HOW TO PROPOSE The *National Encyclopedia of Business and Social Forms*, published in 1879, set forth these principles for marriage proposals: The proposal can be made in writing to the woman's parents, "but it is much better that a personal interview be obtained. The suitor is bound by the paternal decision, whether it is favorable or the reverse." If the suitor is rejected, "it is best for his own and the lady's sake that he should travel for a short time."

In 1969, Adriana Martinez, then 82, and Octavio Guillen, same age, got married in Mexico City after an engagement of sixty-seven years, the longest on record.

On February 29, 1288, Scotland made it legal for women to propose to men. Some believe this to be the origin of

the custom for women to woo men in leap years.

Sir Thomas Seymour proposed marriage to Princess (later Queen) Elizabeth and was so persistent about it that the English government had him charged with treason. He was beheaded March 19, 1549.

CHAPTER 1

IN New Hampshire, joining a religious order disbelieving in marriage is grounds for divorce.

2 World's longest love affair: Adam & Eve, approximately 900 years.

3 Who said, "Love is a devil. There is no evil angel but love"? a) Jimi Hendrix b) William Shakespeare c) Mick Jagger d) Jim Morrison. Answer: *b*, in *Love's Labour's Lost*

4 Though Ellen Sewell was in love with Henry David Thoreau and he with her, she married someone else because her father objected to Thoreau's belief in transcendentalism. Henry apparently never got over Ellen and on his deathbed told his sister, "I have always loved her."

5 Biblical scholars believe the Garden of Eden was located in which country? a) Israel, b) China, c) Egypt, d) United States. Answer: All. Geographic description in Genesis 2:8–14 has scholars theorizing the Garden's location in more than ten locations, including Bristol, Florida.

6 One night after a long, cold, difficult day, Lombardi came home late and tumbled into bed. "God," his wife said, "your feet are cold." And Lombardi answered, "Around the house, dear, you may call me Vince."—A story first told by Vince Lombardi and quoted in *The Book of Sports Quotes* by Bert Randolph Sugar.

7 Religion has done love a great service by making it a sin.
—Anatole France

8 Marriage Encounter weekends were created in the 1950's by a Catholic priest in Spain and have spread to more than fifty countries. The idea grew out of traditional Catholic retreats, but the weekends are open to all faiths. Thousands of couples attend the international Marriage Encounter convention each year. "We had been married for twelve years and things may have gotten a little dull," said one participant at the 1983 convention in Hayward, California. "But the weekend made us realize how important we are to each other. It's more important than my wedding day to me."

$$U_t =$$
$$V(c_t^1, c_t^2, c_{t-1}^1, c_{t-1}^2, c_{t+1}^1, c_{t+1}^2)$$
—Equation devised by Professor Herschel I. Grossman of Brown University to determine the effects of family love on family finances. See *Love & Money* for the title of Professor Grossman's paper on the subject.

Medical science has coined a term to describe a condition in which people fall in and out of love compulsively. What is it?
a) Mononucleosis
b) Antidisestablishmentarianism
c) Hysteroid euphoria
d) Hysteroid dysphoria

Answer: d

Scientist Marie Curie is said to have had an affair with a married scientist who had four children. The people of France were enraged by accounts of the relationship published in the Paris newspapers, and crowds gathered around Mme Curie's apartment shouting insults. When she was awarded her second Nobel Prize, colleagues maintained it was more out of sympathy for her personal problems than for her scientific achievements.

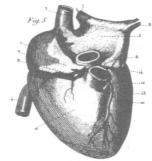
Fig. 5

A Temple University study of 1,800 couples has revealed that twenty-two percent met each other purely by accident in elevators, restaurants, stores, and on streets and buses—instead of through formal introduction, as many people believe.

Senator William Proxmire, as he presented a Golden Fleece Award to a psychologist whose research on love was funded by the government: "I object because no one, not even the National Science Foundation, can argue that falling in love is a science. I'm also against it because I don't want an answer."
—Quoted in the *New York Times*

According to Dr. Michael R. Liebowitz, love may be influenced by our brain chemistry. Falling in love, for example, could have something to do with a natural brain chemical called phenylethylamine (PEA) which has amphetamine-like effects. And endorphins, he hypothesizes, are present when we are in close relationships. Loss of a loved one may shut down endorphin production and throw us into a panic. For more info, consult Dr. Liebowitz' book, *The Chemistry of Love* (Little, Brown, 1983).

I never loved
another person the
way I love myself.
—Mae West

Be a friend to
thyself and others
will befriend
thee. —Kelly

Love is the
need to escape
from oneself.
—Baudelaire

To love oneself is
the beginning of a
lifelong romance.
—Oscar Wilde

In mythology, Narcissus is the youth
who falls in love with a reflection in a
pool—but doesn't know it's his own.

Sex therapist Dr. Theresa Crenshaw (see also *Love & Aphrodisiacs* and *Love & Money*) says that we can create problems in our sex lives just by having unrealistic expectations.

In an interview with *San Diego* magazine, Crenshaw observed that "a woman who takes a long time to come to orgasm is considered frigid, or 'uptight.' A man who takes a long time to come to orgasm is considered a stud, because he can 'keep it up a long time.' A man who comes very easily is considered a 'premature ejaculator.' And a woman who comes easily is considered sexually facile."

Recommended reading: *Bedside Manners*, Dr. Theresa Crenshaw. ♥

Parade magazine reported on a poll that revealed what French men do after they make love: Ten percent make love again, fifteen percent smoke a cigarette, and seventy-five percent go home to their wives.

Shortly after the item appeared, Ann Landers remarked in her column that, "of the seventy-five percent who went home to their wives, I'll bet half of them discovered that their wives hadn't gotten home yet. Two can play that game, and they are doing it more and more." ♥

Why it is that the self often does not only not prefer sex with one's chosen mate, chosen for his or her attractiveness and suitability, even when the mate is a person well known to one, knowing of one, loved by one, with a life, time, and family in common, but rather prefers sex with a new person, even a total stranger, or even vicariously through pornography.
—Title of article on promiscuity in the May 1983 issue of *Vanity Fair*. The article quoted statistics which say only three percent of "swinging" married couples get divorced, compared with fifty percent of those who don't. Monogamy, it theorized, is the result of "cultural constraints...imposed by economic necessities of an agricultural society." ♥

Lovesickness…usually gets diagnosed as depression and then treated with the wrong drugs. The surest prescription is to support lovesick people in therapy for the two years it may take them to recover. They'll know they're over it when they can have a new lover.
—Dr. John Money, quoted in the *New York Times*

Love's not blind, just feeling its way around.
—Frank Rosenhoover

In Rome about 2,000 years ago, the Emperor Tiberius tried to halt a herpes epidemic by banning kissing. ♥

Love paralyzes the joints.
—Botswana proverb

When Brent Deck of Massachusetts started New Day International Social Network in 1982, people with genital herpes thought they were getting a dating service and a major magazine ran the headline, "Herpes Victims Get Matchmaker."

Although New Day does provide a network in which herpes sufferers can meet, Deck emphasizes that "it's not there for people to latch on to the first person who doesn't reject them, but rather for people to form relationships on a normal basis where herpes is not a factor."

New members fill out a ninety-question profile which is identified by a number and circulated anonymously among the organization's members, who numbered almost 1,000 at last count. There's only a charge when members wish to contact each other. For more information about New Day, write P.O. Box 267, Framingham, MA 01701. ♥

Social kissing was popular in England till the late 1600's, when it was replaced with curtsies, bows, and tips of the hat. What happened?
a) It was felt that curtsies, etc., were sexier
b) Mononucleosis, the "kissing disease," broke out
c) The plague broke out
d) The common cold broke out for the first time

Answer: c.

After studying the common cold, a University of Virginia researcher has concluded that its germs are spread more by shaking hands than by kissing. ♥

Who said, "Love is blind"?
a) Chaucer
b) Shakespeare
c) Ovid
d) Gilbert & Sullivan

Answer: a and b, in those exact words, in *The Canterbury Tales* and *The Merchant of Venice*, respectively. Many other writers have said the same thing, though not in the same words.

A DIAMOND IS FOREVER

–ADVERTISEMENT

Seven couples recited
their wedding vows
in front of 15,000 people
in the Atlanta
Fulton County Stadium
in June 1979.
The ceremony took place
on the pitcher's mound
before a Braves game.

The Origin of the White Wedding and Other Traditions
♡ Yellow was the wedding color in early Roman times
and the bride carried wheat ears, symbol of fertility.
In sixteenth-century France, Mary Queen of Scots
defied tradition when she wore white—the mourn-
ing color of French queens—at her own wedding
to the Dauphin of France. Queen Elizabeth I
had red hair and creamy skin, looked smashing
in white, was never married, but prompted
a wave of red-headed brides in   white
dresses. During the American
Revolution brides wore red,
to symbolize rebellion. The
frilly all-white wedding did
not become commonplace
until the nineteenth century
—much more recently than
most people suppose. The Vic-
torian era, says Ann Monsarrat in *And the Bride
Wore....,* "is when it all happened, when the
jig-saw pieces came together to form the great
white wedding tradition." It is also when *bride-
cake* became *wedding cake, bride-men* became
groomsmen, and the *best man* first appeared.

6 LEAST-KNOWN, MOST ROMANTIC SPOTS IN THE WORLD
Contributed by travel writer Walter Houk.

1. **Palawan, Philippines.** Palawan, most difficult and obscure of the major Philippine islands, rewards those who seek it out with beguiling, lush landscapes. You can stay in a good hotel in the sole city, Puerto Princesa, and spend a day or days on a bay full of islets and beaches. You can cross to the South China Sea shore, where an outrigger will take you to the Underground River—a magnificent sea cave thirteen kilometers long.

2. **Africa.** Almost any major game lodge will do, but the Paraa lodge in Uganda offers a climactic boat acquaintance with the swift Victoria Nile. You travel eyeball-to-eyeball with hordes of hippos and gangs of malevolent crocodiles, past a maned lion surveying his domain, in earshot of bellowing elephants. A high-intensity experience.

3. **Islands of Mexican California.** Adventure cruise vessels out of San Diego circumnavigate the peninsula of Baja California and can take you past dozens of almost-deserted islands. The romance is not only in the luxury of a different landing each day, your own private bays, beaches, and sea caves, but in getting close to more marine animals than you'll see anywhere else in the world.

I love you

我愛你

Te amo

4. Machu Picchu, Peru. Remote on a cliff-edged promontory overlooking the mighty Urubamba River, this ruined white city of a brilliant and vanished empire remains as a legacy of poetry in stone. Cross its grassy plaza, contemplate its sacred sundial hewn from living rock. It will hardly seem four centuries since this, one of humanity's most audacious works, was alive.

5. Merced River, Yosemite Valley, California. One of the visual wonders of the planet. In the fall—when crowds have withdrawn—it becomes a hall for a concerto of sensual delights that would have inspired Vivaldi. Lovers never get over its spell.

6. Luxor and the Nile of Upper Egypt. Great rivers are avenues to romance and adventure, and none is more so than the Nile. On the sunrise side at Luxor are monuments of Ramses II and other powerful pharaohs. On the sundown side are funerary temples and tombs, including that of King Tut. At night, the full moon turns the river to silver and you look out past mud-brick houses and date groves—an idyllic scene that has hardly changed in forty centuries.

Ich liebe dich

Ai shite imasu

Je t'aime

Although no serviceman's career was ever *made* by his wife, many have been hindered or helped by the social skills of their wives, their flexibility, and their loyalty toward the Army and its customs....As an Army wife, never forget that you are the "silent" member of the team...You belong to a strong team that has never lost a war.
—*The Army Wife*, manual given to Army wives-to-be before their military wedding.

Who said "All's fair in love and war"?
a) Shakespeare
b) F.E. Smedley
c) Lord Byron
d) Ovid

Answer: b In *Frank Fairlegh*, 1850

Who first said "Love conquers all"?
a) Shakespeare
b) Chaucer
c) Virgil
d) Johnson

Answer: c

Love and war are the same thing, and stratagems and policy are as allowable in the one as in the other.
—Miguel de Cervantes

Horatio Nelson has been named in several polls as one of the top five most beloved heroes of all time. Who was he?
a) British star of the silent screen
b) Admiral who led the British to victory
c) Gandhi's right-hand man
d) George Washington's lieutenant

Answer: b In the Battle of Trafalgar against the French, 1805.

Love is like war: easy to begin but very hard to stop.
—H.L. Mencken

Don't threaten me with
love, baby, let's just go
walking in the rain.
—Billie Holiday

It was so cold I almost got
married.
—Shelley Winters, quoted
in the *New York Times*,
April 1956

Many waters cannot quench
love. Neither can the floods
drown it.
—Solomon's Song, 8:7

What a woman says to her
lover should be written in
wind and running water.
—Catullus, *Odes*

And custom always bears the sway,
If I wont take my sparks to bed.
—Bundling song, eighteenth century

During cold winters in eighteenth century America, "bundling" was a common mode of courtship. An early New Englander wrote: "The parties instead of sitting up, go to bed together; but go to bed with their clothes on. This would appear perilous, but I have been assured of the contrary."

They did it to keep from freezing in log cabins where there was only one fireplace. Housing was improved in the last part of the century, and ministers and social reformers abolished the practice.

Jewell Richbourg of Columbia, South Carolina, was only joking when she mentioned the idea of getting married in the K-Mart store, her place of employment for sixteen years. But fellow workers talked her into it and Richbourg and Phil Priefer were married at the K-Mart luncheonette counter in August 1983.

Betty Lehan Harragan on office romance in her book, *Games Mother Never Taught You:* "Women…must not play this game with any male member of their particular business community if they want to remain viable activists in the impersonal master game of corporate politics where the goal is money, success, and independent power."

What a man *does* with his more than two hundred thousand hours available for work is what gives meaning to his life. Those of us lucky enough to spend all these hours at something we love to do, at something we're good at, are rich.
—George Lois, *The Art of Advertising*

Census data show that approximately one third of all couples with children and dual careers work different shifts.

Corporate counseling programs historically have helped employees cope with alcoholism and drug addiction, but more and more are being established to aid workers with marital problems. Sixty percent of the Fortune 500 companies offer such aid, according to *Money* magazine. Companies are finding it less expensive to improve an unhappy employee's performance through counseling than replacement.

As the number of people without families increases, the workplace becomes more of a home and co-workers more of a family. Even for people with families, work can generate significant emotional bonds. "You are probably more like the people you work with than in many instances you are like the members of your family," said Dr. Carl Eisdorfer, psychiatrist at Mount Sinai Medical Center in a *New York Times* article. "The things you read, the things you talk about, the social events you attend in connection with work —all these give opportunity for warmth and intimacy."

HOW TO BRING MORE LOVE INTO THE WORLD

We asked people all over the world for ideas. Here's what they had to say:

People can be so impatient. Try to be kind. If someone next door wants to get the car out and asks you to hold the baby, you do it. Keep faith in your church. Don't go around preaching, though.
—Iris McCarthy, England

If there's someone you care about, show it. Ideally parents should teach children about love, but maybe schools can, too. Everyone seems to agree that we don't want war. We need to convince the politicians.
—Tina Weinberg, Frankfurt, Germany

Don't isolate yourself. Look for as much contact as possible. And don't try to be too nice by hiding feelings because that hurts.
—Dorine Van Der Schaar, France

More patience. Understanding. Restraint.
—Valery (last name withheld by request), Moscow, USSR

People who get love will give it. It's the ones who don't get it who are bitter. It's best to start at an early age, with parents teaching children to love. There are other ways, small ways. When I'm in charge of dinner and I serve with— what's that Spanish word?—*gusto*—then I'm showing my love.
—Jacob Hope, Kibbutz Nachson, Israel

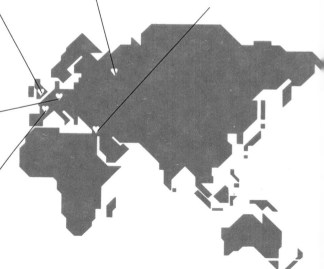

There's no one-liner for this. Love is something you can't get from books or psychology or anyplace outside. It has to be within you and not within your control. It has to come from a spiritual base. If you didn't get it from your parents, if you were dealt a rotten deal, I wish you a lot of luck.
—Bruce Fields, San Jose, California

You have to believe that everything which lives is worth loving. We don't usually think in those terms. You have to love and know yourself. And you have to be genuinely interested in bringing love into the world.
—Pato Castro, Buenos Aires, Argentina

A dating manual in China advises young men to carry a book and a badminton racquet on the first date to convey an impression of intelligence and good health. For women, the manual warns against "the unscrupulous type who rounds corners at full speed on his bicycle."

According to the magazine *Soviet Life*, a poll in the Soviet Union has revealed that what men there want most from a wife is kindness, compassion, and the ability to be a good friend. What women value most in a husband is love of work, intelligence, and respect for others.

Man must evolve for all human conflict a method which rejects revenge, aggression and retaliation. The foundation of such a method is love.
—Martin Luther King, Jr., Nobel Prize acceptance speech

THERE ARE MOTHER♥ AND SELF♥,
FATHER♥ AND CHILDREN'S ♥FOR
THEIR PARENTS; THERE ARE BRO-
THERLY ♥ AND ♥ OF ONE'S HOME
AND ONE'S COUNTRY; ♥ OF MONEY
AND ♥ OF POWER; MAKING ♥ AND
♥ING FOOD; THERE ARE MUSIC ♥
ERS, SPORTS ♥ERS, BIRD ♥ERS, SUN
♥ERS. PREACHERS INSIST THAT WE
SHOULD ♥ GOD. JESUS ADJURES
US TO ♥ OUR ENEMIES…BUT THE
♥ IN WHICH ONE CAN BE IS THE
PRE-EMINENT ♥ FOR MOST OF US.

—Julian Huxley, *Look*

We welcome reader contributions.
If you have a fact, saying, list
or story about love to share for our
next volume or calendar on the subject,
please send it to The Book of Love
in care of the publisher.
Be sure to include exact sources,
and your name and address.

L.L. and P. S.